CW01266100

THE NAME OF GOD

PREPARING FOR THE MONTH OF RAMADAN

God's Banquet

Author: Ali Reza Panahian
Translator: Hoda Shirvani
Editor: Gail D. Babst

Preparing for the Month of Ramadan: God's Banquet

Author: Ali Reza Panahian

Researched and Edited by:

The Asr Bayan Manavi Institute

Translator: Hoda Shirvani

Editor: Gail D. Babst

Published by: Bayan Manavi, Tehran, Iran

Publishing date: April 2021

Website: Panahian.net

Email: salam@panahian.ir

ISBN: 979-873-28416-4-0

Contents

A NOTE FROM THE PUBLISHER 9

Chapter 1

BANQUET 11

- What is a banquet?
  - What can we understand from this notion of "being guests"?
  - A banquet is temporary: Benefitting from it
- The Ramadan banquet
  - Spiritual speculations about the Ramadan banquet
  - The reason why giving Ifṭār to people who are fasting brings many rewards
  - Moments spent with the Friends of God
- A banquet by force
  - The philosophy of a banquet by force
  - The sweetness of being forced
  - A discussion about the obligatory deeds a guest must do and giving hardship to a guest in the Ramadan banquet

Chapter 2
PERMISSION TO ENTER 35
- Worries surrounding our entry
  - The Messenger's (s) words about the difficulty of adhering to the etiquettes of the month of Ramadan
  - Missing the excellent opportunity provided by Ramadan
  - Worries surrounding our entry
  - Why aren't some people worried whether their deeds will be accepted or not?
- The sweetness of entering
  - The newness of the month of Ramadan has a freshness
  - Feeling a need for becoming close to God
  - Don't God's Friends get tired of being with God?
  - The banquet for God's Friends: An opportunity for satisfying their endless needs

NOTES 53

REFERENCES 59

A Note from the Publisher

Being prepared before entering any banquet helps a person to enter that banquet with more peace of mind and enthusiasm. It also allows us to benefit more from that banquet, which is waiting for us. The book, which is in your hands, is in fact the first part of the book "The Month of Ramadan and the Secrets of Fasting." In this book, some practical points about fasting have been discussed in a simple, pleasant language. It prepares the reader to enter a spiritual atmosphere with a fondness for the month of Ramadan. Furthermore, it provides the opportunity for people who will be fasting to establish a deeper relationship with the innermost parts of this banquet, which we may have ignored up to now, and to enjoy and benefit from attending this banquet more.

We hope this book will be helpful in strengthening your spiritual relationship with the month of Ramadan, God's banquet.

Chapter 1

Banquet

- What is a banquet?
- The Ramadan banquet
- A banquet by force

WHAT IS A BANQUET?

Saying that the month of Ramadan is a banquet [Ḍīyāfat] is perhaps the most important description of Ramadan. If we want to explain the nature of Ramadan, we should start with this description, which is the most fundamental description of this dear month. Ramadan means a banquet; it is the month of God's banquet. In Ramadan, we are God's guests and He is our Host. Although we were God's guests from the beginning of creation and have always benefited from His blessings, in the month of Ramadan we are His guests even more than before. What is the message for us behind this extra, special way of being His guests? What subtle meaning is this term supposed to convey to us about the month of Ramadan?

Describing Ramadan as being a banquet is not just some term that men of letters and mystics chose to their own liking. Rather, it is the term the dear Holy Prophet (s), who is aware of all the realities in the world, used when talking about the month of Ramadan. The Prophet (s) used this term in referring to Ramadan in the beginning sentences of the *"Sha'bāniyah Sermon,"* where he said, "You have been invited to God's banquet in this month."[1] Therefore, we should pay attention to the particularities of this term and description. We should use the opportunity this metaphor has given us to gain the utmost understanding about the month of Ramadan.

What can we understand from this notion of "being guests"?

First, we need to see what can be understood from the notion of being guests. Especially if we want to interpret the topic of being guests according to the culture of our own religion, we should investigate what special characteristics it has. We should also refer to our own hearts and see how we feel when we hear a discussion about being guests or when we think of the relationship between a host and a guest. This is what the kind Prophet (s) wants us to understand and feel from the month of Ramadan.

A guest is dear and should be honored even if he/she is an unbeliever. Our Holy Prophet (s) said, "Honor a guest even if he/she is an unbeliever."[2] A banquet is the place for kindness and abundance. If the host is generous and honorable himself, he pays attention to the meaning of a banquet when honoring his guest. He doesn't consider how deserving his guest is when serving him. Similarly, the host does not think the high position and status of a guest is something to cause him to be proud. The host considers his own hospitality to be something honorable. The reason we have been told to even honor unbelievers when they are our guests is due to the fact that having guests is honorable in itself. Those who have relayed this command to us have definitely adhered to this better than anyone else.

In a banquet, relationships have a new, special meaning, and the guests are usually friendly with each other. The competitiveness that often exists between people for gaining more usually changes into a balanced relationship and mutual understanding. The reason for this is that everyone is being served and in order to be given more, one must go to the host. If the host is wealthy, there is no need to be worried about any shortages.

Apart from the fact that the guests are friendly with each other, the relationship between the guest and the host is also a new, special relationship. If the guest has done something wrong in the past, the host will not be harsh with him or reprimand him based on what he has done before. The guest won't be admonished or monitored because of his past faults. Everyone knows that a banquet is not the place for such admonitions.

People's status and level change in a banquet. Without the honor of people of a high standing being reduced, people at a lower level will be honored and exalted too. Everyone comes closer together. Even if there is a distance between the guest and the host, the guest feels that he is close to his host. Being a "guest" is something in itself that brings honor for whomever it is applied to. This title brings a special dignity in the same way that titles such as brother, friend, or relative do.

If a guest helps, he will be thanked twice as much. If he rests and does not help, he is still valued and honored. On the other hand, the host is not concerned about being appreciated and praised. In the process of serving his guests, he is only thinking about benefiting his guests and is not considering his own profit. He becomes happy when his guests smile and constantly asks them if they have had enough to eat.

If a host does not have a need for guests or for inviting people to a banquet, and he serves his guests in a suitable way, then we can say that the host's intention is nothing but to serve his guests and honor them. The less need the host has for others, the more he will show his abundant affection and munificence. If a person gives a banquet only because of his kindness while he has no need for the guests or for holding a banquet, his action will have a beautiful effect. This beautiful effect is due to the fact that his only reason for holding this banquet is because of the beauty that will be created. We can sometimes see such beauty described in the stories of mysticism.

If the host is a great dignitary and the guests are at a much lower level than him, when he holds a banquet it will be the place for the manifestation of the host's humbleness. The moments when a host with great dignity is humble in front of his guests are memorable, cherished moments. Being the guest of a highly dignified person makes ones dignified too and removes humiliation from one's soul - the humiliation that is the cause for all enslavement.

If the host is a popular, lovable person, participating in his banquet seems like an unreachable dream. If the guest loves the host to the extent that he even considers his broken dish to be a sign of the love of his beloved [as is descried in the story of Leyli and Majnun][3], he will almost die [from happiness] when the host is serving him. Imagine someone who is in love. He is willing to wait patiently behind the door of his beloved his whole life grieving and sighing even though the beloved is ignoring him. How will he feel when his beloved opens the door, lets him in, and allows him to sit in the most honored place in the house?

A banquet is temporary: Benefitting from it

A banquet is temporary and is an occasion that we are only passing through. With all its beauties and sweetness, it is just a passageway. One should know its value and appreciate it. One should endeavor to benefit from this opportunity appropriately. There is no time for negligence in a banquet. One should be attentive, benefit from participating in it, and pay attention to its moments. Of course, there are times when the guest ends up staying in the host's house and becomes like a member of the family, such as when the banquet is being given as part of a gathering for a bride and groom. Another example is when a banquet results in one catching a glance of someone and falling in love. An inner feeling is manifested and brings a new closeness. So the guest becomes a part of the family. In previous banquets, you were at the same level as this person and eating from the same table with him. But the next time you see him, he is beside the host. He is welcoming and serving you in the same way that the host does. Yes, these things happen in a banquet too. Guests like us who have just arrived cannot be compared with the new hosts who have become settled in that house.

The minimum benefit one receives from a banquet is not being alone and feeling lonely. At the same time, sorrows are washed away too. Going to a banquet means coming out of the repetitive, boring environment of one's own home and entering the beautiful manor where the banquet is being held. A banquet is an opportunity for enjoyment and variety. It is an opportunity for meeting the people who are dear to us and who bring relief and love. Talking and spending time with these dear, good people is one of the splendid benefits of such a banquet.

Of course, all of these depend on who has invited you and what your situation is. Depending on your eagerness and the host's goodness, your mannerisms and the host's welcoming you, your sorrow and the amount the host removes that sorrow, and your love and the host's behavior, banquets will differ from each other. In general, it depends on you yourself and how you view the banquet of the month of Ramadan.

THE RAMADAN BANQUET

Now let's review our understanding and feelings about Ramadan using the outlook that we have now gained about a banquet. The Holy Prophet (s) introduced Ramadan in the Sha'bāniyah Sermon. After describing the month of Ramadan as a "banquet," he talked about what is "served" or given in this banquet, "God honors you in this month to such an extent that even your breathing is counted as remembering Him and your sleeping is counted as worshiping. Your deeds are accepted, and your prayers are answered."[4] We couldn't be "served" or honored any more than this. It is obvious that what God "serves" or gives in this banquet are spiritual matters, which are very much in accordance with the goal of this banquet.

Spiritual speculations about the Ramadan banquet

I do not want to repeat all that has been said so far about a banquet. Comparing the similarities between a banquet and the month of Ramadan is up to you. What we want to do is to continue thinking about what has been said. We want to let our feelings flourish so that in the process of pondering over this dear banquet, our spiritual speculations may illuminate our hearts and sight even more.

Perhaps the month of Ramadan is an opportunity for becoming familiar for those of us who are strangers, who are far from remembering God and being close to Him, and who are not familiar with the status of the ones who are familiar and in love with God. So if we do not become familiar with God in this banquet, when will be able to work on ourselves and become real human beings?! When we are not able to experience being with the Host when we are present in His house, how will we be able to experience this when we are not in His house?!

Maybe the month of Ramadan for those of us who are familiar with God is a place where God wants us to see ourselves closer to Him because of this banquet. After each period of negligence or sin, the first setback that strikes us is that we think God does not care about us or love us anymore. We think He won't look at us anymore. No one is able to convince us that God is always concerned about us, He loves us and He is still with us. Maybe the environment of the banquet will be able to correct our belief about God's kindness and make us more hopeful about improving ourselves.

With each sin, the first harm we inflict on ourselves is that we become "hopeless" about God's mercy. We ourselves close the way to being able to return to Him. Without doing something to deserve it, we can still be "hopeful" of being served well and feel honored due to God's munificence in this banquet. This in itself causes us to gain many virtues, and it is a wealth for us with many benefits.

Maybe we are going to be "Muḥtaram" (honored) in this banquet so that we will feel a little that we are "Maḥram" (intimate) and consider sins to be "Ḥarām" (forbidden) for ourselves. This is similar to what happens when people go on Hajj. As soon as they enter God's House, they go into the state of "Iḥrām" (and put on the special white clothes prescribed for Hajj). Similarly, we are going to become "Muḥrim" (certain actions will become forbidden), and we will not be "Maḥrūm" (deprived)" from joining the good people. Maybe this is telling us that we are able to become "Maḥram" to know the secrets and come close to the Lord. [All of these words: Muḥtaram, Maḥram, Ḥarām, Iḥrām, Muḥrim and Maḥrūm come from the same Arabic root word.] Since we frequently do not consider ourselves to be honorable people, we do any and all actions, right or wrong. Since we think we are incapable, we do not try to take any action to correct ourselves.

Another purpose of a banquet is to help us to not feel distant so that we won't try to escape from the Host. As a result, we will find some peace when being with Him. God waited for us to go toward Him on our own during the year, but we didn't. Therefore, He has invited us Himself to create an intimacy and to remove our fear. In this way, this good memory will take us back to Him in order to repeat this sweet experience in the future.

At the same time, it is also possible that the Host wants to show the extent of His generosity and how kind He is to His servants so that we too will show that we deserve to be His servants and to be forgiven by Him. He wants to display His Lordship to us, and He wants us to display our worshiping and flying to the height of His dignity to the angels. This display is captivating from

Him and beautiful from us. Witnessing these beauties is only possible for pious, religious people.

Perhaps the banquet is to eliminate our solitude and loneliness. God is well aware that when we are far from Him, we feel forlorn and there is a commotion going on within us. At the same time that a banquet is the start of a new understanding and familiarity for some people, it is also a healing for the pain of love and devotion for some other people.

Maybe He wants us to distance ourselves from others a little so that we can somewhat understand our loneliness in order to be able to eliminate some of the impurities that we have gained through our relationships with others. In other words, He wants us to become fond of Him, and the sign of being fond of God is distancing our heart from others. About this, the Commander of the Faithful, Ali (as), said, "The result of becoming fond of God is fearing [that we may become fond of] people."[5]

It is possible that one reason for this banquet is for us to become more familiar with each other. When we human beings become totally separated from each other, it is as if we become distanced from ourselves too. And when our hearts become closer together, it is as if we come to our senses a little and as a result it will be easier for us to become closer to God. When we are arrogant toward each other, our humbleness toward God will decrease too. When we are kinder to each other, God will also be kinder to us. In a banquet where the guests are gathering around the host, in fact, they have gathered in a congregation and so they become closer to each other too. Of course, this is not contradictory to the loneliness that was mentioned previously.

The Prophet's (s) instructions about how the believers should be kind to each other in this banquet is surprising. It is as if the purpose of this banquet is only for the guests to become friends again and the whole reason for this banquet is for them to be kind to each other.

The Prophet (s) said, "Give charity to the poor and needy. Honor your elders and have mercy on the children. Do good to your relatives. Control your tongue. Prevent your eyes from looking at that which is prohibited. Prevent your ears from hearing that which is forbidden. Be kind to the orphans of others so that others may be kind to your orphans.

O people, whoever corrects his temper in this month will pass over the 'Ṣirāt Bridge' on the day when feet slip on it [in the Hereafter]. If a person is easy on his dependents and subordinates, God will be easy on him when calculating his deeds. If a person stops himself from doing evil to others during this month, God will prevent His wrath from reaching him on the Day of Judgment. If a person honors an orphan, God will honor him on the Day of Judgment. If a person is good to his relatives, God will be good to him on the Day of Judgment. And if a person cuts off his relations with his relatives, God will cut off His mercy from him on the Day of Judgment."[6]

The reason why giving Ifṭār to people who are fasting brings many rewards

Maybe one of the reasons that giving Ifṭār [or food for breaking one's fast] to people who are fasting brings many rewards is because of the very important benefit that comes from this banquet. About this the Holy Prophet (s) said, "O people, whoever gives Ifṭār to a fasting believer in this month will receive the reward given to a person who frees a slave, and his past sins will be forgiven too."[7]

Some people said, "O Prophet of God, we don't have enough money to give Ifṭār." The Prophet replied, "Protect yourself from the Hellfire, even if it's with half a date. Protect yourself from the Hellfire even if it's with a sip of water."[8] This means that you now have a good opportunity where you are able to remove the effect of all past sins with such a simple act. So distance yourself from the Hellfire, even if it is with a single date or a bowl of water.

I do not know if giving one date for Ifṭār is that valuable. This does not feel right. Maybe God wanted to declare how dear a fasting person is. If you give even a little food for him to break his fast and are kind to him, God will forgive your sins. How could God announce that He loves His fasting guest and honors him any more than this?

Moments spent with the Friends of God

Probably the main purpose of this banquet, or in other words, the main benefit of this banquet is that we can be with the Friends of God for a few moments. They have always been close to Him, are God's servants, are dear to Him, are the ones who bring the food in this glorious banquet, are the ones who bring a pure drink, and are responsible for serving the guests. At the same time, they are intimate with the Host and constantly remembering Him. [These Friends of God are intermediaries who bring God's grace.] Otherwise, God is always with us and we are always His guests.

It is as if He wants to reduce the distance between us and his Special Friends so that we can find the way using their light and walk in their presence. In addition, He manifests Himself in our hearts by way of their existence and attracts us by way of these beloved ones. By showing the Guardians (Imams), He wants to express His purpose in guiding us and revealing the Qur'an. And by having us follow the school of thought of Guardianship (Imamate), He is completing His favour upon us.

This is so that God may test us with our love for them, and also so that they may help us to love God. It is so that we may find these role models that we had lost, and for them to see us next to themselves so that they may caress us with their grace. We are greatly in need of them. But more than that, they are eager for us.

If the previous statements are incorrect, why is the "Night of Destiny" (Qadr) during this banquet the night when the Qur'an was revealed all at once?

Isn't the revelation of all these verses at once like God showing His Guardians to the entire population of the world? Then, God can say, "[My Guardians are the manifestation of the Qur'an, and] this is what I wanted to show." If this is incorrect, why should all of the servants' - I mean the guests' - affairs and destinies for the whole year be signed by God's Guardian during this night, and why should he be aware of these? Why did the Commander of the Faithful (as) say, "I am the daily prayer and fasting of the believers"?[9]

The answer to these ineffable words is clear. However, one should do more research concerning these topics by studying the discussions about Guardianship. So for now, let's leave this topic. You should refer to yourself and test yourself on this subject, and you will easily see that during this Ramadan Banquet, you feel closer to the Household of the Prophet (as) and are more fond of them. So keep yourself beside them and do not wander away from them, or else, it will be to your loss.

A BANQUET BY FORCE

When showing the similarities between two things, there is no need for both of the two sides to be completely alike and we can sometimes overlook the differences. However, let's examine these differences between the Ramadan banquet and other gatherings and benefit from learning about these differences too. People sometimes compare two things so that they can benefit from paying attention to their differences and they mention their main points when talking about these differences. Let's see if we can do this in this case too.

There are at least three basic differences between the month of Ramadan and the common gatherings we are familiar with. Along with all the goodness that exists in Ramadan, Ramadan is a banquet by force and it is not optional. But is it possible for a banquet to be by force? With the passing of time, you will inevitably enter this banquet [with the start of the month of Ramadan according to the Lunar calendar]. This force of nature is something that exists for everyone. And this is the first difference.

In addition, in this banquet the Host forces the guests to obey religious legislation by making fasting compulsory and commanding them to fast. But it is not common to compel a guest to do something. And this is the second difference.

The third difference is that since fasting is obligatory, which means tolerating not eating or drinking, this banquet involves special hardships that are not common.

O God, You are holding a banquet, so why have you made it obligatory to participate in this banquet, which is filled with kindness? You could have said anyone who is interested can come, like Iḥrām during the recommended Hajj [`Umrah al-Mufradah] and I`tikāf [religious seclusion or spiritual retreat in the Mosque]. However, this banquet has been designed in such a way that no one is allowed to not enter it. Since this banquet is held at a certain time in the year, we will enter this time whether we wish to or not and whether we benefit from it or are negligent about it. The month of Ramadan is not like I`tikāf or Hajj where a person's will is important and it depends on his/her wanting to participate.

The philosophy of a banquet by force

Why should a banquet be by force? The answer to this is very clear. Sometimes a person who likes his friend very much invites him to his gathering with such insistence that it is as if he does not want his friend to have a choice in this matter, and he takes him to his gathering by force. For example, he says, "You must come tomorrow. No excuses accepted! Be ready at such and such time, and I'll pick you up by car myself. Bye!" If he likes him even more, he'll say, "If you don't come, that's it!"

In fact, God says, "O human beings, whether you want to or not, whether you are awake or asleep, the month of Ramadan, My banquet, will come and surround you with its blessings and mercy. You are forced to participate in My banquet and gathering." God's natural laws compelling everyone to enter this banquet (and enter the month of Ramadan) is due to His intense interest in inviting His servants. God likes to invite His servants so much that He has made it compulsory to participate in this banquet and has not given people the opportunity to decide about this themselves.

The God Who always waited for us to go toward Him ourselves, does not wait for His servants' decision and action in this month. By making Ramadan a period that everyone must enter, it is as if He has come toward His servants Himself, grabs everyone's hand and takes them toward His mercy.

Of course, God is showing His magnanimity. Great people behave in this way with people at a lower level very frequently. Unfortunately, it is true that in today's world, we do not see a positive relationship between great people and people of a lower level very much. When we do hear about a relationship between great people and people of a lower level, since we human beings are all equal and this kind of relationship leads to oppressing others, it is not an attractive, positive relationship. But when God, who is truly great, is kind to a being at a lower level, this is not bitter. It is actually very sweet.

A banquet by force is a combination of both the Almighty God's affection and His greatness toward His servants. God has given us enough freedom and choice in order for us to become good. But at the same time, we should realize that we have ruined ourselves and accept for God to pull us one step toward Himself, although He will release us again a little while later.

If a person thinks that it would have been better if this banquet were based on people's choice, he should come at the end of this month to prevent the people who have fasted and the guests who have participated in this banquet by force from their crying and grieving when saying farewell to this month. When he sees their behavior and sadness, how can he account for this much feeling of gratitude on the part of the guests toward the Host?

The sweetness of being forced

It is not true to say that force is always something bad. Sometimes, if force is accompanied by deep affection, it is something beautiful in the lives of us human beings. We can see this kind of behavior in the relationship between mothers and their children very much.

Of course, if we want to speak more accurately about this, we should look at the truth of the relationship between the Master and His servant and see what is so appealing about the Master for the servant. Does a servant expect his Master as much as he expects his friend even though the Master loves the servant very much? In Persian it is said, "It is befitting for a lion to attack and for a gazelle to escape." We should not think that "behaving well" and "behaving affectionately" are always the same thing and so ask for both.

Of course, we should talk about this subject in more detail at another time and explain the truths behind the relationship between the Master and His servants. That which befits a Master is to command and force, and that which befits a servant is being submissive. The Master does not consult with His servant, does not leave him to choose, and He talks to him as a magistrate would, whether it is a law in nature or religious legislation, as in this case, and the Master is manifesting His Guardianship and patronage. What moments could be more appealing for a servant than seeing the manifestation of this Guardianship?

Even in the moments when the Master frees His servant from His natural laws and His religious commands, the servant tolerates those moments patiently while waiting for the moments when he will be a captive again.

Actually, a servant tries to make all the moments when he is free to choose similar to the moments when he is forced to obey the commands of his Master. That is why he obeys Him so much, does not sin and is constantly trying to understand his duty. Those who have tasted the pleasantness of obeying Him have experienced the sweetness of all this in themselves.

A discussion about the obligatory deeds a guest must do and giving hardship to a guest in the Ramadan banquet

The previous explanation about the first difference between the Ramadan banquet [a banquet by force] and other banquets also applies to the second and third differences [obligatory deeds the guest must do and giving hardship to the guest]. Fasting being obligatory is a religious command, which is a manifestation of God being God. It is true that we have less authority with regard to the laws of nature for natural development, and people can only rebel with regards to the divine, obligatory commands. Nevertheless, the obligatory commands and the laws of nature are similar to each other in that they are both by compulsion. According to what has already been stated, that which is obligatory for us whether they are religious commands or laws of nature are much more valuable and more appealing in comparison to recommended commands. You can fast the whole year, but why is it that this is not as pleasant as fasting in the month of Ramadan?

In fact, God has invited us to participate in the month of Ramadan with both His laws of nature by way of the passing of time and with the divine command for fasting. He, as God, serves us in this Banquet. What Banquet could be higher than this? In order to make it clear that this is a divine banquet for His servants – and that this is what He wants - He has commanded us to fast. In this way, He gives a command, which is against the nature and natural needs of human beings, so that the manifestation of the relationship between the Master and His servant - which is the truth of this banquet - may be seen better.

We will not talk about the benefits and effects of fasting here. These benefits should be discussed at another time and place. In another discussion we should consider the "command to fast" and the questions, "What are the natural benefits of fasting?" and "How does hunger refine a person's nature preparing him/her to benefit from the spiritual banquet of the month of Ramadan?" This question should also be discussed, "Why is it that eating too much is in contradiction with spiritual uplifting?"

Participating in the month of Ramadan is obligatory for everyone, whether they are willing to do so or not. And fasting and tolerating hunger are divine obligatory commands that must be carried out. These are all some of the prerequisites to a mystical gathering and banquet, which not everyone is allowed to enter. In order to participate in that, one must tolerate many hardships. So not everyone is allowed to enter and participate in it.

Although participating in this public banquet is obligatory and may seem easy in the beginning, being in that private banquet is actually by choice and is difficult. In order to be able to enter that private banquet, the good people in the world supplicate and beseech God very much.

Chapter 2

Permission to enter

- Worries surrounding our entry
- The sweetness of entering

WORRIES SURROUNDING OUR ENTRY

With all its goodness and beauty, the month of Ramadan has caused us to become God's guests and God is our Host. Now, how should we feel about this? How should our heart feel when approaching the month of Ramadan? Due to all the divine, good promises, should we go toward Ramadan only with delight and happiness? Or should we have a certain amount of fear too?

There is no doubt that the enthusiasm that is due to the joy of being allowed to enter such a generous banquet is the first thing that comes into one's mind. However, if fear and enthusiasm come together, fear usually shows itself first. It is as if fear says, "First rid yourself of me, then hasten toward that which you are enthusiastic about." You well know that fear arises from the middle of enthusiasm. Due to our enthusiasm for pleasure, we should fear that which is frightening and approach it rationally.

If we believe we are in the presence of the Host (God) in this banquet and also understand God's Greatness, without a doubt we will be worried about not being respectful enough with regard to this glorious court while being desirous of this banquet at the same time. Even before leaping to participate in this general gathering, fear of the manifestation of that boundless grandeur in comparison to our smallness will stream into our being.

Imam Sajjād (as) said in his supplication in bidding farewell to the month of Ramadan, "[O month of Ramadan,] how great you were in the eyes of the believers."[10] Where does this greatness come from? Naturally, this grandeur is due to getting close to the Lord. And, it is due to the importance of adhering to the etiquettes and doing the important deeds of the month of Ramadan so that one will not be impolite toward His Holy Being or toward His holy, gracious banquet.

The Messenger's (s) words about the difficulty of adhering to the etiquettes of the month of Ramadan

The Prophet of God (s) told Jābir bin `Abdullāh about the blessings of the month of Ramadan, its conditions and its etiquettes. He said, "O Jābir, this is the month of Ramadan [that has arrived]. Whoever fasts during its days, arises and worships a part of its nights, keeps his stomach and desires away from what is forbidden, and prevents his tongue [from evil], will leave his sins behind [and be purified] as he leaves this month."[11]

Jābir became happy when he heard the sweet promises about the month of Ramadan and said, "O Prophet of God, what beautiful words!"[12] He was referring to this announcement about the month of Ramadan. However, the Prophet of God (s) said, "O Jābir, these conditions are very difficult."[13] In fact, the Prophet (s) was emphasizing the hardship of adhering to the etiquettes of Ramadan and wanted to pull Jābir's attention to the significance and importance of Ramadan. It is clear that the Prophet of God (s) wanted his good followers to not just be drowned in enjoying the blessings of Ramadan and to be concerned about being careful to adhere to the etiquettes of Ramadan too.

Of course, we should understand some aspects of the hardships of the month of Ramadan from the term "banquet." Because no matter how many blessings a person receives in a banquet, he cannot be as comfortable as when he is in his own home. Due to the need to behave politely, he is not as comfortable as when he is in his own home. Even if a person is having great fun when participating in a banquet, he cannot behave just any way he wants. Due to the importance and grandeur of the banquet, he thinks of benefiting from it more than he thinks of his own comfort.

Missing the excellent opportunity provided by Ramadan

Isn't the month of Ramadan an excellent opportunity? Aren't we very eager and in need of it? So we should be worried that we may not make the best use of this opportunity and not find tranquillity in it. The dearer this banquet is to us, the more we are worried about wasting it [and not making the best use of this opportunity]. These uncertainties cause us to ask endless questions, such as the following.

Are we going to benefit in the best way from this month? Are we going to be one of those who do not gain anything from fasting except hunger during this holy month of Ramadan? Will our many needs be fulfilled in this month? There are so many other similar questions to these, which only come to the minds of ambitious, eager people.

This is true unless we are so overflowing with spiritual blessings already that we do not feel an urgent need for any more, and the blessings of Ramadan are mostly just an entertainment and amusement for us. This talk is so absurd and baseless that one should not even think of it. Although it is not at all hard for the Friends of God to satisfy Him, they beseech the beneficent God so much for a small amount of His grace. This shows the situation of other people [and how much they should beseech Him].

However, I should say that in this case our situation is one of the following two. Either we are concerned about mysticism and worshiping, or we are not. If we are not concerned, it is quite clear how much we are in need even if we ourselves do not realize this. And if we are concerned about these, we have probably already become so interested in God's blessings and kindness that we plead with a great feeling of need in order to receive more of His grace and kindness.

Worries surrounding our entry

Let's review briefly some of our worries along with the reasons for these worries.

The first point to be made is that truly good people like to do everything correctly. They do not like their "works of art" to be defective. Our actions in the month of Ramadan each year are like a "work of art" that will remain from us in the universe. We will even see this work of art in the Hereafter. Even if our actions in the months of Ramadan in later years are good, they will not make up for the deficiencies in this month of Ramadan. Each time is a separate work of art.

Being worried that we may not be able to spend the month of Ramadan in the best way is a common worry for such people. This is the least factor, which creates some worries for them and accompanies their enthusiasm.

Secondly, the month of Ramadan is typically the peak of our spirituality, and we are not usually in a better situation at other times outside the month of Ramadan. In comparison with any score we get in the month of Ramadan, our score will probably be lower at other times. We may be worried that the spiritual height we are flying at may not be high enough, and that the zenith of our spirituality not be enough. This is the second matter that severely worries ambitious people who are not negligent of this matter.

The third point is that the more holy and dear Ramadan is for those who love God, the more it will cause them to worry about if they will be able to respect and be grateful for this great blessing. It is obvious that each of these worries has its own "flavor," or feeling. Some of these worries, like this one, are not bitter or repulsive. It is actually appealing and sweet. This is similar to the situation of someone who is in love and who is worried about taking good care of a gift that he has for his beloved so that it won't be damaged. Thus, he protects it rigorously.

The fourth worry is about us being forgiven in the month of Ramadan. Being forgiven is so important that the Prophet of God (s) said, "Wretched is the one who is deprived of God's forgiveness in this great month."[14] Doesn't this worry us that we may not be forgiven and our bad points may not be pardoned and passed over? If this happens, we may leave Ramadan with the same bad traits. So when will the vices that have not been washed away with the pure water of Ramadan be cleansed?

The fifth worry concerns the fact that the month of Ramadan is the month of worshiping, and our worship acts will be presented to God, the Almighty. Won't His greatness and the grandeur of His position be a reason for us to be worried about our deeds being of too little value? Won't being worried about our deeds being accepted due to His high degree cause us servants to be continuously concerned?

Why aren't some people worried whether their deeds will be accepted or not?

When some people worship God, for example when they pray, they are not at all concerned about whether God will be satisfied with their worship acts or not. Some people are not concerned if their fasting in this Ramadan will be satisfactory or not. On the other hand, they have such concerns about many other affairs in life. Excuse me for saying this, but it is as if they feel God owes them and He has oppressed them by forcing them to do this worship act. Therefore, they believe that this little amount of worshiping that they are doing is even too much for the One Who has given them this command.

They do not know that God first looks at how His servants feel. If a person is not worried about his deeds being accepted, it is as if he is doing them reluctantly. How valuable are such deeds to God?

In every deed that a servant does – before, during and after that deed - God wants His servant to show enthusiasm for Him and love Him. When God sees that His servant sends his worship acts toward Him negligently and is not worried whether his deeds will reach Him and be accepted or not, such deeds are not valuable to Him. Therefore, the benefit that some people receive from the month of Ramadan is only being hungry and thirsty for a month.

This is like a hired hand who has been oppressed and forced to dig the ground. After digging the ground, such a person does not look into the eyes of the employer to see if he is satisfied. He only looks at his hands in anticipation of his wages. If he thinks the employer will not pay him at all because he is so oppressive, he will throw the shovel in front of the employer and leave.

Do you know when it is that people like us are not worried about the results of our deeds and are not worried whether our deeds will be accepted or not? If anyone is trying to refrain from accepting what has been said, I would like to say one last thing. I want to give an example, and I offer you my apologies beforehand.

Consider the example of a poor person who comes to our door wearing tattered clothes. We want to give him something to eat. If we do not care about him and if that which we want to give him is something extra that we have at home, we won't care about the dish we use or the food that we give him. We won't think about whether he will like it or not. This is especially true if we do not expect him to return the dish. In this case, we are not worried about our deed being liked. We only wish to give him something to get rid of him.

Without a doubt, finding relief from these concerns and others that haven't been mentioned here, cannot come about without the Almighty God's help. In the same way, a person won't be concerned unless he has knowledge of and love for the Worshiped One.

A person who is worried about the results of his deeds from the beginning is looking from above. Such a person recites this prayer from the Qur'an with a loving, mystical fear when entering the month of Ramadan, "And say: My Lord, make me to enter a goodly entering, and cause me to go forth a goodly going forth, and grant me from near Thee power to assist (me)."[15]

THE SWEETNESS OF ENTERING

Let's put aside all the worries and concerns surrounding our entering this month, along with the many things that can be said about this. Let's start talking about some of the other feelings that the guests of the month of Ramadan experience when entering this month. The start of the holy month of Ramadan and entering the banquet of the kind God, in addition to creating an enthusiasm in a person, also has an obvious sweetness.

It seems this holy month automatically bestows a special spiritual status and a sweet feeling of worshiping on a person, which one should appreciate very much. In order to appreciate it, we should first do something very simple. We should put time to enjoy this sweet beginning the most we can. That's it.

We should drown ourselves in this spiritual joy as much as we can, so that we may make the best memories for ourselves and the people around us by using this opportunity. Then, when we aren't in such a situation in the future, this memorable experience can take us back to those pure, spiritual moments and be a tool for us to return to God.

One reason for the sweetness of the start of the month of Ramadan is the memories that have remained for us from previous years. The sweet voice that recites the supplications at the time for breaking the fast each year and which reminds us of the sweet memories of previous years is one of the signs of this sweetness that we have created for ourselves during this beautiful opportunity at the start of Ramadan. And this has great benefits for us too.

The newness of the month of Ramadan has a freshness

One very simple reason for this sweetness that we experience is that Ramadan is new each year and this in itself creates a liveliness and freshness in a person. Ramadan is not like our daily prayers that sometimes become boring and something routine for us due to their repetitiveness. Although it is not enough to like and enjoy Ramadan just because it is new, it is not bad either. We should appreciate these small opportunities in order to not be deprived of the greatest opportunities.

It is difficult to "be friends with God" for most of us who do not have that much knowledge and who have not stopped being fond of this world. However, renewing our covenant and our relationship has always been something sweet and appealing, like the sweet moments when we are first becoming familiar.

We should use the energy we gain from this being something new to benefit from it, not for the far future, but for the middle of the month of Ramadan when that energy that we have in the beginning is gone. By planning from the beginning of the month of Ramadan, by having a special plan for worshiping for the various times during this month, by doing the special worship acts for this month of Ramadan, by using that beginning energy and also changing our regular program, we should gain the most benefit from that beginning vitality.

In the same way that in the beginning of the holy month of Ramadan something called "being new" gives vitality and happiness to a person, in the following days, something called "a feeling of fondness" is created within a person, and one can taste a different sweetness. Of course, the sweetness that comes from this feeling of fondness is a much deeper feeling than the sweetness that is created in a person's heart as the result of something being new. In order for this beginning sweetness to continue and for it to become a feeling of fondness, one should be hard on him/herself a little and resist in the face of his/her own initial reluctance.

Feeling a need for becoming close to God

Another reason for the sweetness of entering the dear month of Ramadan is the feeling of needing to be close to God, which is understandable only when a measure of closeness has been achieved. It is at this time that a person understands how bitter it was to be far from God.

The warm feeling of God's love and mercy can be felt easily in the beginning due to the amount of coldness that one was experiencing previously due to neglecting Him. Then, a person gradually understands how cold and spiritless he truly was outside of God's kind, warm embrace.

It is as if we human beings gradually get used to living without God and being far from Him, or at least we do not feel much of a need for being close to God. But, as we step into God's good month again, we strongly remember how much we need His affection.

We are like a playful child. A child is busy playing when his mother is absent. As soon as he sees his mother, he remembers his need for her caresses and hurries to her embrace crying. But a little later, after he has found peace being in her warm, kind embrace, he again starts looking around and searches for a new toy to play with. He goes toward the worthless toys outside of his mother's kind embrace and forgets that he ran from these toys to his mother just a few minutes ago.

The difference is that a child needs to play in order to grow. Neglecting his mother's kindness makes the mother's job easier too. But even a foolish person understands that we need God's kindness in each and every moment. This should not be something that only takes place in this banquet. Neglecting His caresses is not beneficial to us. Any game that separates us from Him is a dangerous, destructive game, and its harms should be taken seriously.

Unfortunately, some people can only feel good about meeting their old acquaintances when they meet them again after a long time. On the contrary, gentle people miss their friends very quickly. Some people cannot delay making up for very long after they have had an argument with someone. Similarly, the tender heart of God's Friends cannot tolerate being far from God. They want to talk to God at least five times a day. They feel they cannot do anything unless they talk to God very much.

Don't God's Friends get tired of being with God?

Now I ask you, "How will this group feel when the month of Ramadan starts? Does God's banquet in Ramadan feel repetitive for them since they are always with God? Is Ramadan new only for those who are strangers or have pouted? Do you think like some people with little knowledge do, who believe that if we are with God very much, we will gradually get tired of Him? Do you think like ignorant people do by asking, 'Don't those who are always with God need variety and entertainment?'"

Actually, this is a common mistake and a false understanding. Many people think that the religious believers are always able to be with God since they have let go of experiencing variety, entertainments and many natural joys that human beings need. They have abandoned this world. Thus, the reward they gain in the Hereafter is due to the suffering they tolerate due to "being with God." Such people, who do not have much experience in behaving in accordance with their religion, think that having knowledge about God means that same rudimentary understanding that they have about God. They think the believers constantly repeat the same rudimentary concepts to themselves without experiencing any new feelings or understanding!

Using deep, mystical words, Imam Ṣādiq (as) said, "If people were aware of the virtues and value of having knowledge about the Almighty God, they would not be desirous of the beauties and blessings that God has given to their enemies. Furthermore, their life in this world would have been even more worthless to them than the dust under their feet. They would enjoy having knowledge of God so much that it was as if they were with God's Friends in Heaven's gardens. Indeed, having knowledge of God is like experiencing having an intimate person with us who does not allow any fear to remain in us. Whenever a person is alone, this intimate person is his comrade. Having knowledge about God illuminates any darkness, removes any weakness, and cures any illness."[16]

The banquet for God's Friends: An opportunity for satisfying their endless needs

The truth is that only those who are always with God and have a banquet going on within themselves at times outside the month of Ramadan too are able to truly taste being present in this banquet.

Actually the banquet is being held for them and all other people are off to the sides of this banquet. This banquet is for fulfilling the needs of the people who are always with God. From the corners of this table, which is filled with blessings, other people can benefit too.

Rewards for deeds being doubled in the month of Ramadan is actually for filling the endless, spiritual capacity of such great, luminous people. It is as if their tender hearts cause prayers to be answered more in the month of Ramadan. Since their wings are wider than to be able to fit in the narrow space of this world, and flying and soaring high is not possible for them that easily in a normal situation, the doors of the skies open to them in this month.

That is why Ramadan is called the Eid of the Friends of God. Imam Zayn al-`Ābidīn (as) said, "Salam to you, O God's greatest month and the Eid of His Friends."[17]

This is the third reason for the happiness and excitement we feel at being in the month of Ramadan, and this is only for God's Friends. Not many people are able to truly taste this pure experience. But if hearing that God's Friends are happy is sweet for us and causes us to wish to taste such moments, this is enough for us for now and it is a good sign.

God's Special Friends start this month with an extra excitement and passion from the very first day. They are completely familiar with this month. They know what they should do during this month. They know where they should go. They know who they should spend time with. They do not wander about curiously. Their enthusiasm for this month is not due to it being a new experience. No, they open their wings and soar in this month!

Nonetheless, when you look at their faces, you can see the sorrow of the last day of Ramadan in their tears of happiness. "Salam to you, O month which the hearts ask for (and are awaiting) before it arrives and which the hearts become sad for (and miss) before it ends."[18]

Such people do not neglect the fact that this month will finish even though they still have some time left in it. From the very first day, they are like people who are experiencing the last moments of this month, and their only hope is that God will enable them to benefit from this month. Their hope is in God from the first day, the One Who bestows on the last day, and so they are not proud of their ability to worship Him and their skill in obeying Him.

Notes

Chapter 1

1. This is a tradition from the Holy Prophet of God (s). [`*Uyūn Akhbār al-Riḍā*, vol. 1, p. 295, chapter 28, tradition no. 53. *Mafātīḥ al-Jinān*, Refer to the discussion on the virtues of the holy month of Ramadan.]

«هُوَ شَهْرٌ دُعِيتُمْ فِيهِ إِلَى ضِيَافَةِ اللهِ.»

2. This is a tradition from the Holy Prophet of God (s). [*Jāmi' al-Akhbār*, p. 84, section 40.]

«أكرِمِ الضَّيفَ وَلَو كَانَ كافراً.»

3. This is referring to the story of the love of a young man named Majnun for a young woman named Layli. One time Layli broke Majnun's dish and Majnun considered this to be a sign of her love. It is common to refer to love stories in Farsi literature when talking about the love between God and His servants in order to make this love easier to understand. [Trans.]

4. This is a tradition from the Holy Prophet of God (s). [`*Uyūn Akhbār al-Riḍā*, vol. 1. p. 295, chapter, 28, tradition no. 53.]

«وَ جُعِلْتُمْ فِيهِ مِنْ أَهْلِ كَرَامَةِ اللهِ.»

5. This is a tradition from Imam `Alī (as). [*Ghurar al-Ḥikam*, p. 199, the section "Fī `Ibādah Allah," tradition no. 3,949.]

«ثَمَرَةُ الْانسِ بِاللهِ الإستِيحَاشُ مِنَ النَّاسِ.»

6. This is a tradition from the Holy Prophet of God (s). [`*Uyūn Akhbār al-Riḍā*, vol. 1, p. 295, chapter 28, tradition no. 53.]

«وَ تَصَدَّقُوا عَلَى فُقَرَائِكُمْ وَ مَسَاكِينِكُمْ وَ وَقِّرُوا كِبَارَكُمْ وَ ارْحَمُوا صِغَارَكُمْ وَ صِلُوا أَرْحَامَكُمْ وَ احْفَظُوا أَلْسِنَتَكُمْ وَ غُضُّوا عَمَّا لَايَحِلُّ النَّظَرُ إِلَيْهِ أَبْصَارَكُمْ وَ عَمَّا لَايَحِلُّ الِاسْتِمَاعُ إِلَيْهِ أَسْمَاعَكُمْ وَ تَحَنَّنُوا عَلَى أَيْتَامِ النَّاسِ يُتَحَنَّنْ عَلَى أَيْتَامِكُمْ

أَيُّهَا النَّاسُ مَنْ حَسَّنَ مِنْكُمْ فِي هَذَا الشَّهْرِ خُلُقَهُ كَانَ لَهُ جَوَازاً عَلَى الصِّرَاطِ يَوْمَ تَزِلُّ فِيهِ الْأَقْدَامُ وَ مَنْ خَفَّفَ فِي هَذَا الشَّهْرِ عَمَّا مَلَكَتْ يَمِينُهُ خَفَّفَ اللهُ عَلَيْهِ حِسَابَهُ وَ مَنْ كَفَّ فِيهِ شَرَّهُ كَفَّ اللهُ عَنْهُ غَضَبَهُ يَوْمَ يَلْقَاهُ وَ مَنْ أَكْرَمَ فِيهِ يَتِيماً أَكْرَمَهُ اللهُ يَوْمَ يَلْقَاهُ وَ مَنْ وَصَلَ فِيهِ رَحِمَهُ وَصَلَهُ اللهُ بِرَحْمَتِهِ يَوْمَ يَلْقَاهُ وَ مَنْ قَطَعَ فِيهِ رَحِمَهُ قَطَعَ اللهُ عَنْهُ رَحْمَتَهُ يَوْمَ يَلْقَاهُ.»

7. *Ibid.*

«أَيُّهَا النَّاسُ مَنْ فَطَّرَ مِنْكُمْ صَائِماً مُؤْمِناً فِي هَذَا الشَّهْرِ كَانَ لَهُ بِذَلِكَ عِنْدَ اللهِ عِتْقُ نَسَمَةٍ وَ مَغْفِرَةٌ لِمَا مَضَى مِنْ ذُنُوبِهِ.»

8. *Ibid.*

«اتَّقُوا النَّارَ وَ لَوْ بِشِقِّ تَمْرَةٍ، اتَّقُوا النَّارَ وَ لَوْ بِشَرْبَةٍ مِنْ مَاءٍ.»

9. This is based on an interpretation of verse 115 in Chapter Baqara. [*Tafsīr Anwār al-`Irfān*, vol. 2, p. 533.]

«اَنَاْ صَلوةُ الْمُؤمِنينَ وَ صِيامُهُم.»

Chapter 2

10. *Ṣaḥīfah Sajjādiyah*, supplication no. 45, "Bidding Farewell to the Month of Ramadan."

«وَ [ما] أَهْيَبَک فِی صُدُورِ الْمُؤْمِنِينَ.»

11. This is a tradition from the Holy Prophet of God (s). [*Kāfī*, vol. 4, p. 87, Refer to the chapter "Adab al-Ṣā'im," tradition no. 2.]

«يَا جَابِرُ هَذَا شَهْرُ رَمَضَان مَنْ صَامَ نَهَارَهُ وَ قَامَ وِرْداً مِنْ لَيْلِهِ وَ عَفَّ بَطْنُهُ وَ فَرْجُهُ وَ كَفَّ لِسَانَهُ خَرَجَ مِنْ ذُنُوبِهِ كَخُرُوجِهِ مِنَ الشَّهْر.»

12. *Ibid.*

«يَا رَسُولَ اللهِ مَا أَحْسَنَ هَذَا الْحَدِيثَ.»

13. *Ibid.*

«يَا جَابِرُ وَ مَا أَشَدَّ هَذِهِ الشُّرُوطَ.»

14. This is a tradition from the Holy Prophet of God (s). [*`Uyūn Akhbār al-Riḍā*, vol. 1, p. 295, chapter 28, tradition no. 53.]

«فَإِنَّ الشَّقِيَّ مَنْ حُرِمَ غُفْرَانَ اللهِ فِی هَذَا الشَّهْرِ الْعَظِيمِ.»

15. *Qur'an*, 17:80.

«وَقُل رَبِّ اَدخِلنِی مُدخَلَ صِدقٍ وَ اَخرِجنِی مُخرَجَ صِدقٍ وَ اجعَل لِی مِن لَدُنک سُلطَاناً نَصِيراً.»

16. This is a tradition from Imam Ṣādiq (as). [Kāfī, vol. 8, p. 247, the section "Al-Rawzah," tradition no. 347.]

«لَوْ يَعْلَمُ النَّاسُ مَا فِی فَضْلِ مَعْرِفَةِ اللهِ عَزَّ وَ جَلَّ مَا مَدُّوا أَعْيُنَهُمْ إِلَی مَا مَتَّعَ اللهُ بِهِ الْأَعْدَاءَ مِنْ زَهْرَةِ الْحَيَاةِ الدُّنْيَا وَ نَعِيمِهَا. وَ كَانَتْ دُنْيَاهُمْ أَقَلَّ عِنْدَهُمْ مِمَّا يَطَئُونَهُ بِأَرْجُلِهِمْ وَ لَنُعِّمُوا بِمَعْرِفَةِ اللهِ جَلَّ وَ عَزَّ وَ تَلَذَّذُوا بِهَا تَلَذُّذَ مَنْ لَمْ يَزَلْ فِی رَوْضَاتِ الْجِنَانِ مَعَ أَوْلِيَاءِ اللهِ. إِنَّ مَعْرِفَةَ اللهِ عَزَّ وَ جَلَّ آنِسٌ مِنْ كُلِّ وَحْشَةٍ وَ صَاحِبٌ مِنْ كُلِّ وَحْدَةٍ وَ نُورٌ مِنْ كُلِّ ظُلْمَةٍ وَ قُوَّةٌ مِنْ كُلِّ ضَعْفٍ وَ شِفَاءٌ مِنْ كُلِّ سُقْمٍ.»

17. This is a part of a supplication from Imam Sajjād (as). [*Ṣaḥīfah Sajjādiyah*, supplication no. 45, "Bidding Farewell to the Month of Ramadan."]

«اَلسَّلامُ عَلَیکَ یا شَهرَاللهِ الأکبَرِ وَ یا عِیدَ اَولِیائِهِ.»

18. *Ibid.*

«السَّلَامُ عَلَیْکَ مِنْ مَطْلُوبٍ قَبْلَ وَقْتِهِ، وَ مَحْزُونٍ عَلَیْهِ قَبْلَ فَوْتِهِ.»

References

1. `Allāmah Ṭabāṭabāī, Sayyid Muḥammad Ḥusayn. (1374 AHS). *Tafsīr al-Mīzān*. Mūsavī Hamidānī, Sayyid Muḥammad Bāqir (Trans.), Qum, Iran: Daftar Intishārāt Islāmī.

2. Āmudī, `Abdulwāḥid bin Muḥammad Tamīmī. (1366 AHS). *Ghurar al-Ḥikam Wa Durar al-Kalim*. Qum, Iran: Daftar Tablīghāt Islāmī Ḥawzah `Ilmiyah Qum.

3. Dāvar Panāh, Abulfaḍl. (1375 AHS). *Tafsīr Anwār al-`Irfān Fī Tafsīr al-Qur'ān*. Tehran, Iran: Intishārāt Ṣadr.

4. Imām `Alī bin al-Ḥusayn, Imām Sajjād (as). (1376 AHS). *Ṣaḥīfah Sajjādiyah*. Daftar Nashr al-Hādī.

5. Kulaynī Rāzī, Abū Ja`far Muḥammad bin Ya`qub. (1365 AHS). *Al-Kāfī*. Tehran, Iran: Dār al-Kutub al-Islāmiyah.

6. Shaykh Ṣadūq, Abū Ja`far Muḥammad bin `Alī bin Ḥusayn bin Bābawayh Qumī. (1378 AHS). *`Uyūn Akhbār al-Riḍā*. Intishārāt Jahān.

7. Shaykh Ṣadūq, Abū Ja`far Muḥammad bin `Alī bin Ḥusayn bin Bābawayh Qumī. (1413 AHL). *Man Lā Yaḥḍuruh al-Faqīh*. Qum, Iran: Mu'assisah Intishārāt Islāmī.

8. Shu`ayrī, Muḥammad bin Muḥammad bin Ḥaydar. (1363 AHS). *Jāmi` al-Akhbār, Shaykh Tāj al-Dīn*. Qum, Iran: Intishārāt Raḍī.

9. Markaz Mu`jam Fiqhī Wa Markaz Pazhūhishhāyi Islāmī al-Muṣṭafā. 1384 AHS. *Kitābkhānih Ahlulbayt (as)* (1). [Computer Software]

10. Markaz Taḥqīqāt Kāmpyūtirī `Ulūm Islāmī Nūr. *Ganjīnah Rivāyāt Nūr*. [Computer Software]

11. Markaz Taḥqīqāt Kāmpyūtirī `Ulūm Islāmī Nūr. *Jāmi` al-Aḥādīth* (2). [Computer Software]

12. Markaz Taḥqīqāt Kāmpyūtirī `Ulūm Islāmī Nūr. *Jāmi` Tafāsīr*

Nūr (2). [Computer Software]

13. Markaz Taḥqīqāt Kāmpyūtirī `Ulūm Islāmī Nūr. *Mu`jam Muḍū`ī Biḥār al-Anwār.* [Computer Software]

Printed in Great Britain
by Amazon

19525229R00038